# A MANUAL OF
# ORGANIZATIONAL
# DEVELOPMENT

# A MANUAL OF ORGANIZATIONAL DEVELOPMENT

## The Psychology of Change

*Clare Huffington, Carol Cole,*
*& Halina Brunning*

London
KARNAC BOOKS

Published in 1997 by
H. Karnac (Books) Ltd.
58 Gloucester Road
London SW7 4QY

Based on *The Change Directory*, published by
The British Psychological Society, 1990

Illustrations by Kristof Bien.

**British Library Cataloging in Publication Data**

A C.I.P. record for this book is available from the British Library

ISBN: 1 85575 128 3

Edited, designed, and produced by Communication Crafts

10 9 8 7 6 5 4 3 2 1

Printed in Great Britain by BPC Wheatons Ltd, Exeter

# ACKNOWLEDGEMENTS

We would like to acknowledge the many authors and practitioners in the world of organizational behaviour on whose work we have drawn. Our material has been derived from a variety of sources and, whenever possible, these have been attributed. However, it has not always been possible to trace the geneses of all our ideas.

We would, therefore, like to take this opportunity to acknowledge all those whose work, in one form or another, has influenced or enriched our thinking and hence contributed to this manual.

# CONTENTS

# ABOUT THE AUTHORS

**CLARE HUFFINGTON** M.Sc., P.G.C.E., AFBPsS, C.Psychol.

A Chartered Psychologist working as a Consultant to organizations in the public and private sectors. She is a Senior Consultant with the Tavistock Consultancy Service, which specializes in working with the human side of organizational change; in particular addressing psychological processes beneath the surface—in individuals, in groups, and in the organization as a whole—which can get in the way of fundamental change.

Clare has developed consultancy training for managers, consultants, and human resource professionals in a variety of organizations. She has written a number of articles and six books on consultancy, organizational change, and related topics.

**CAROL COLE** MA Hons, M.Sc., PhD, AFBPsS, C.Psychol.

An independent consultant in Organization Development with extensive experience in the United Kingdom and overseas in both the public and private sectors, including the health, oil, and communications industries.

Carol has worked as a Change Management Consultant with the National Health Service and as an Organization Consultant with Shell International, for whom she continues to consult. Recent assignments have included the implementation of major cultural changes, structural reorganizations, quality management initiatives, and business process re-engineering.

Carol is an Associate of Ashridge Management College and a visiting Fellow at the Office for Public Management. She has a PhD in Behaviour Change and is a Chartered Clinical Psychologist.

 **HALINA BRUNNING** MA (Clin.Psych), AFBPsS, C.Psychol.

A Chartered Clinical Psychologist, currently with Richmond, Twickenham, and Roehampton Healthcare NHS Trust. Her activities include managing the Psychology Department, teaching, training, supervision, and running staff work reflection groups.

Halina works as an Internal Consultant to projects within her own organization and as an External Consultant for projects within the public sector, specializing in Away Days for team-building and reviews. She has written several papers and two books on the subject of consultancy and has organized numerous training events and courses on consultancy.

**Associated joint papers by the same authors**

*The Change Directory—Key Issues in Organizational Development and the Management of Change*, The British Psychological Society, 1990.

Huffington C., & Brunning H., *Internal Consultancy in the Public Sector: Case Studies*, Karnac Books, 1994.

# FOREWORD

Organizations are now experiencing massive changes and for prolonged periods. Whether we observe this as customers, clients, suppliers, employees, or managers, we know that the changes are not superficial. By the end of this millennium, organizations that are fit to survive will need to learn how to transform themselves continuously in order to adapt to, and shape, their environments.

Managing the processes of change is complex. It requires an understanding of the messy, emotional aspects of transition. The best plans can go astray when people do not embrace change and are not helped to manage their feelings about it. Successful management of change requires attention to both the "what" and the "how" of change.

In managing change and organizational development, executives may find it hard to step outside the organization's current culture, and so they get caught up in "improving what we already do", rather than reviewing "what else we should be doing". Managers therefore often seek help from consultants, so that they can move to a new frame of reference and begin to imagine new possibilities. Consultants may be involved from initially facilitating the formulation of the strategic plan, through to the process of implementation.

If managers intend to work with a consultant, they need to understand what it is that the change process demands and what the consultant can offer. This is not easy for the manager, who has the dual task of specifying what the consultant is to do, whilst not producing such a tight brief that the consultant cannot exercise her or his expertise. For consultants and human resources professionals, too, the task is daunting. How can they keep abreast of current thinking and explain to their internal and external clients exactly what their role is and what benefit they can bring?

This manual is designed to fill this need. It provides an understanding of the nature of organizational change and how this needs to be addressed. It provides a map of how managers and other professionals can work together to achieve success. The roles of change agents and consultants is explained. How they can assist in the formation of new organizations, with flatter, leaner structures, is explored. Key issues in making these changes work in practice—for example, making teams effective and empowering staff—are incorporated.

This book is written in a down-to-earth style in a form that makes these complex concepts accessible to managers, consultants, and human resources professionals. The text is alive with diagrams, tables, and graphics, so that information is available at a glance. The authors also know that many readers will be fascinated with this topic and want to follow it up; the end section provides a directory for further sources of information and assistance.

The authors are all experienced psychologists as well as consultants. This puts them in an excellent position to provide the reader with a practical guide to the essentials of organizational change without avoiding the difficult issue of guiding people through the process of transition. For those with responsibility for facilitating and actioning organizational change, this updated and extended edition of the manual will provide an invaluable asset.

Dr. Kim James, B.Sc(Hons) Ph.D. C.Psychol. MIPTD. AFBPsS
Senior Lecturer in Organisational Behaviour
Cranfield School of Management
Cranfield University

# INTRODUCTION

## WHAT IS THIS MANUAL ABOUT?

This manual is about Organization Development, an exciting and growing field of applied behavioural science with far-reaching implications for organizations, for their clients or customers, and for those who work in them.

## WHOM IS THE MANUAL FOR?

Organizations in the 1990s are in a state of permanent change, and therefore managers, consultants, and human resources professionals need to know how to understand and work most effectively within this constantly changing environment.

Those professionals who are called upon to implement organizational change need a ready reference to issues that they must consider and skills that they must develop to take on the change management role effectively.

## WHAT ARE THE AIMS OF THE MANUAL?

- to introduce basic concepts of organizational function and development
- to outline some key skills in the successful management of organizational change
- to provide a framework in which various models and methods of organizational consultancy can be integrated
- to examine the role of the internal and external consultant in the management of change
- to offer information for further research.

# CHAPTER 1

# THE WORLD OF CHANGE AND ORGANIZATIONS

Global changes & mega-trends

Organizations in transition

# ● GLOBAL CHANGES & MEGA-TRENDS

It is a truism to state that society in general—and organizations in particular—are currently experiencing profound and wide-reaching change. The only certainty is uncertainty itself, and, with quantum changes and discontinuities in all aspects of life, the world of tomorrow will not be like the world of today.

The various commentators on this global upheaval agree that we are in the midst of a significant and sharp transformation, where worldview and values, political and social structures, arts and institutions are all altering in ways that are difficult to predict (see Figure 1.1).

The impact will be felt across infrastructure, science and technology, the environment, health and medicine, education and training, lifestyle, work, and business. The contingent challenges and opportunities may include:

- the likely emergence of three distinct world groupings (the Americas, Eurafrica, and Greater Asia/Australasia)
- the creation of small nation-states
- the globalization of the market-place
- the growth in power of regional and transregional agencies
- the impact of IT: "thinking local, acting global"
- the international mobility of management and professional people
- the rise of the "green" consumer and concern with conservation and pollution
- the promise of biotechnology and genetic engineering
- more business alliances, partnerships, and joint ventures
- the delivery of quality, design, and service
- the currency of "knowledge" as the basic economic resource.

**FIGURE 1.1   The changing environment**

| Old | | New |
|-----|---|-----|
| industrial society | → | information society |
| national economy | → | world economy |
| forced technology | → | high tech/high touch |
| standard products & services | → | tailored products and services |
| uninformed customers | → | demanding customers |
| initial qualification | → | continual updating |
| single discipline | → | multidisciplinary |
| lifetime practice | → | mobile careers |
| employment or self-employment | → | portfolio careers |
| perpetual succession | → | temporary arrangements |
| cartels, barriers, and oligopolies | → | competition and choice |
| relatively few and similar | → | multiplicity and heterogeneity of bodies |
| diversification | → | focus |
| institutional help | → | self-help |
| representative | → | participatory |
| hierarchies | → | networks |
| facts and theories | → | values |
| attitudes | → | feelings |
| quantity | → | quality |
| procedures | → | processes |
| individuals | → | groups and teams |
| getting ahead | → | achieving balance |
| absolutes | → | relative/contextual |

# • ORGANIZATIONS IN TRANSITION

Those individuals and organizations most likely to survive and thrive on these mega-trends are what Kanter (1995) calls "world-class"—cosmopolitans rich in three intangible assets:

- **concepts**—the best and latest knowledge
- **competence**—the ability to operate at the highest standards of any place anywhere
- **connections**—the best relationships, providing access to the resources of other people and organizations around the world.

And yet there is

> "... no single formula or image. ... Multiple possible futures, the need for discontinuity almost for the sake of it, means that we must be able to think imaginatively, to be able to develop ourselves and, in generative relationships with others, to organise and re-organise ourselves continuously."
>
> [Pedler, in Fisher & Torbert, 1995]

The challenge for organizations (*and* for individuals and groups) is therefore in moving beyond the environmental turbulence and in dealing with organizational transitions by **learning** and **actively managing change**.

> "For an organisation to survive, its rate of learning must be equal to, or greater than, the rate of change in its external environment."
>
> [Revans, in Garratt, 1987]

But where does this leave us? Such learning and change management, if they are to be successful, do not simply happen: they need careful orchestration.

"It is not enough to look at what excellent organisations and managers are already doing. It is also necessary to be proactive in relation to the future: to anticipate some of the changes that are likely to occur and to position organisations and their members to address these new challenges effectively."

[Morgan, 1988]

This is where the world of organizations—and organization development—comes in.

# CHAPTER 2

# ORGANIZATIONS AND ORGANIZATION DEVELOPMENT

What is an organization?

Core elements of an organization

Organizational dynamics

The effective organization

The healthy organization

The learning organization

What is organization development?

OD interventions

# ● WHAT IS AN ORGANIZATION?

"Every enterprise has four organizations: the one that is written down, the one that most people believe exists, the one that really exists, and, finally, the one that the enterprise really needs."

[Turrill, 1986]

There are, of course, numerous perceptions of organizations. The personnel specialist may view it as a large organization chart with staff numbers and job descriptions. To the engineer, it may be a collection of machinery, plant, and equipment in need of maintenance and repair. The accountant may see it in terms of profits, losses, and balance sheets, while the clinician may think in terms of patient services and coping with multiple demands.

While each perspective is in itself valid and real, it is only part of the picture; there is a clear need to take a "helicopter" view of the totality of an enterprise and its activities (see Figure 2.1). The elements of the model in Figure 2.1 are discussed further in the next section.

## FIGURE 2.1    A model of organizations

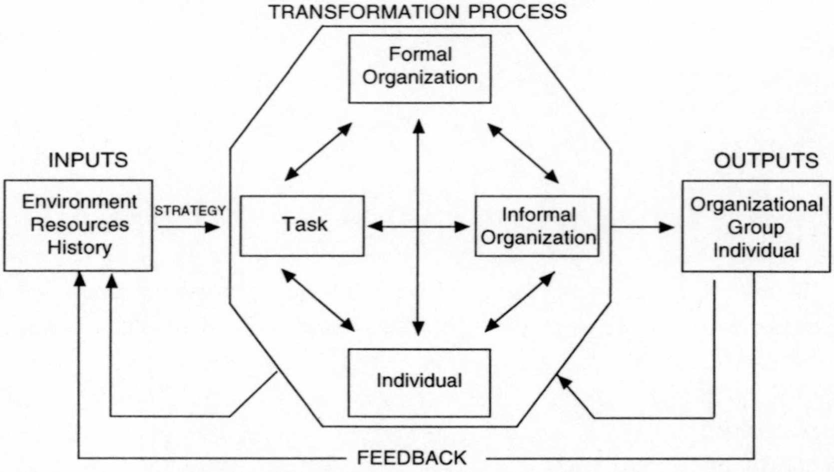

[From D. Nadler & M. Tushman, "A Diagnostic Model for Organization Behavior." In: *Perspectives on Behavior in Organizations*, edited by J. R. Hackman, E. E. Lawler, & L. W. Porter. New York: McGraw-Hill, 1977. Reproduced by permission of the publisher.]

# ● CORE ELEMENTS OF AN ORGANIZATION

## INPUTS

An organization's **environment, resources, history**, and **strategies** together define how people in the enterprise behave, and these factors function as "setting conditions", i.e. constraints as well as opportunities.

## The environment

Many of the demands made on an organization emanate from outside the organization itself. Thus the *raison d'être* for most organizations is to meet such demands, e.g. to provide a service for clients. It is therefore essential that an organization understands the demands that it is there to satisfy.

## Resources

Resources can be tangible assets such as capital (equipment, finance, property, etc.), technologies, and people, and intangibles such as reputation or image.

## History

Because people have memories of an organization's past, their experiences will influence their current and future patterns of behaviour. Similarly, the whole organization as an entity in itself will have a sense of history, which influences, for instance, its traditions, norms, policies, the sort of people it attracts and recruits, and even how crises are typically resolved.

## Strategy

Strategy describes the process of defining how an enterprise's resources can be best deployed for optimal organizational effectiveness. It involves the identification of opportunities in the environment and an awareness of the organization's strengths and weaknesses.

# THE TRANSFORMATION PROCESS

The transformation process consists of four major interactive components:

- **The formal organization**

  This refers to the "structure" of an enterprise—organization charts, policies, procedures, information systems, monitoring and control mechanisms. These are the "hard" features used to organize the work to be done.

- **Task**

  Given that the organization exists in order to pursue a purposeful human activity, the tasks are the actual jobs to be carried out.

- **Individuals**

  Because organizations are composed of people, different individuals bring differing knowledge and skills, as well as differing needs to be satisfied. However, there has to be a means of organizing them so that the organization's tasks are accomplished. This then requires a balance between the needs of the individuals, the way they are formally organized, and the tasks they have to perform.

- **The informal organization**

  This is the "softer" or social aspect of an organization, which gives meaning to those who work in it. It oils the formal structure, and includes the "culture" of the enterprise.

Organizational culture is an especially powerful determinant of behaviour. It refers to a system of shared values ("what is important") and beliefs ("how things work") that interact with the other three transformation components—structure, tasks, and people—to produce behavioural norms ("the way we do things round here").

## OUTPUTS

Outputs can be considered at each of three levels: organizational, group, and individual.

At the holistic level, output reflects:

1. how well the enterprise is achieving its objectives, be they service or production, etc.
2. how it is deploying its resources
3. how it is coping with its environment.

At the group and individual levels, these three concerns similarly apply, but they may be measured differently, e.g. in terms of inter-departmental collaboration or individual job satisfaction and performance.

## FEEDBACK

Any organization may be considered a living entity, i.e. in a constant state of growth or development. Its "outputs", whether at the organizational, group, or individual level, will in turn constitute part of that organization's environment, its resources, and its history. In this way, it is taking in new information about itself and adjusting its behaviour in a feedback loop.

## ● ORGANIZATIONAL DYNAMICS

The Nadler and Tushman model of organizational activity in Figure 2.1 (which is only one such model) applies whatever an organization's size or "boundary" (be it a company, a team, or an individual), as does the following definition:

> "An organization consists of (usually) a group of individuals organising themselves to meet some kind of need, demand or expectation".

> [Nadler & Tushman, 1977]

However, while such definitions and models are helpful, it is important to remember that an organization is never static. Instead, it operates within a *dynamic* equilibrium. When an external change inevitably occurs, the organization can either continually react, or else it can proactively anticipate and adapt to such change and so learn to manage its future development.

These different ways of behaving are portrayed in Figure 2.2, in terms of immediate or future time perspectives and inner or outer locus of control.

**FIGURE 2.2. Dynamic equilibrium**

| | | TIME PERSPECTIVE | |
|---|---|---|---|
| | | Operational (immediate) | Strategic (future) |
| **L O C U S  O F  C O N T R O L** | Reactive (outer) | **Focus:** immediate problem<br>**Function:** symptom relief<br>**Liability:** absence of big picture | **Focus:** anticipation & preparation<br>**Function:** coping & strategy development<br>**Liability:** overlook immediate needs |
| | Creative (inner) | **Focus:** desired results<br>**Function:** innovative products<br>**Liability:** overlook proven processes | **Focus:** anticipation of vision/purpose<br>**Function:** define and design the future<br>**Liability:** failure to reality test |

[after Adams & Spencer, 1986]

- **TIME PERSPECTIVE**

  **Operational perspective**: Focuses on **immediate** concerns, short-range implications, and management. Emphasizes analysis, correction of deviations, and maintaining consistency. Usually this is the normal (socialized) perspective.

  **Strategic perspective**: Focuses on **future** outcomes, long-range implications, and leadership. Emphasizes catalyzing changes, prevention of problems, and the establishment of new directions. Usually this perspective must be consciously adopted.

- **LOCUS OF CONTROL**

  **Reactive thinking:** Responds to **external** stimuli, authorities, and constraints. Emphasizes responding, logical and agreement formation. Usually this is the normal (socialized) mode of thinking.

  **Creative thinking**: Arises from **internal** stimuli and personal preferences and standards. Emphasizes initiative taking, intuition, and the establishment of commitment. Usually this mode of thinking must be consciously adopted.

## ● THE EFFECTIVE ORGANIZATION

While different modes will be appropriate in different settings, organizations that include a strategic proactive approach in their repertoire are these days more likely to survive and to succeed. That is, they will more readily survive environmental turbulence and succeed in meeting demands made of them, simply because their activities will be more integrative, purposeful, and hence effective.

It is worth clarifying here what we mean by effectiveness, as opposed to, say, efficiency. **Efficiency** is really the ratio of input to output, as in "miles to the gallon". **Efficacy**, another associated concept, represents the *way* in which activities are carried out—irrespective of good fuel consumption, is a car the best means of making the journey? Finally, at the level of **effectiveness**, is the journey worth making?

Associated with this notion of organizational effectiveness are several other similar descriptions, namely, the **Healthy Organization**, the **Learning Organization**, and the **Developing Organization**.

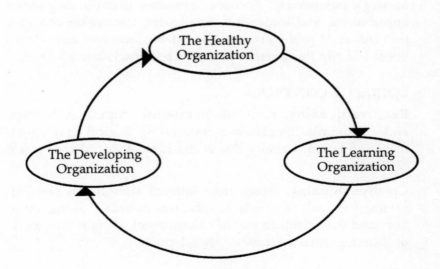

# ● THE HEALTHY ORGANIZATION

In the modern world, organizations can easily become monuments to past thinking rather than the most appropriate configuration for the realities of the present and the challenges of the future.*

> A Healthy Organization is one that values the best possible match of **Purpose, Structure, Process, Resources, Reality,** and **Relationship with the Environment**.

## Purpose

A healthy, effective organization tends to be purposeful and goal-directed. The leadership of the organization, the heads of functions and programmes, and individual units and people have, in addition to day-to-day interests, some relatively explicit goals and directions towards which they are working.

The development of a purpose is important in that it creates a focus with which people can identify, it provides a framework for understanding the whole and linking together the various levels and sub-units, and it provides criteria for resource allocation.

## Structure

Form follows function. The organization chart, the ways in which work is organized and resources allocated, and the location of decision points are defined by the work requirements, not by the authority or power requirements. Power is widely dispersed and differentiated from (official) authority.

---

*This section is based on an MIT working paper entitled "Characteristics of a Healthy Organization", by Richard Beckhard; see also Beckhard & Harris, 1987.

## Process

Decisions are made based on location(s) of information, rather than roles in the hierarchy.

Communication is relatively open. The norms (or ground rules of the system) reward differences of opinion on ideas, solutions to problems, goals, etc., regardless of the authority relationship of the "differers".

Inappropriate competition is minimized; collaboration is regarded where it is in the organization's best interests.

Conflict is managed—neither suppressed nor avoided. The management of conflicts over ideas, work, etc. is seen as an essential part of everyone's job.

## Resources

There is a conscious effort to support each individual's identity, integrity, and freedom. Work and rewards are organized to maintain these.

The reward system(s) are related to the work to be done—attention is paid to intrinsic, as well as extrinsic, rewards, e.g. the lower-paid supervisor's work is no less valued than the higher-paid manager's work.

## Reality

There is an "action research" mode of behaviour. The organization sees itself as always "in process"—needing to have mechanisms for collecting information on the state of things and consciously planning improvements. There are built-in "feedback mechanisms" ("how are we doing?") at all levels.

There is a constant awareness of the values, beliefs, and assumptions used in the organization, of the position of the organization in its life cycle, and of the constraints and controls on the organization's inputs and outputs.

## Environment

The organization is seen as an open system, embedded in a complex environment, the parts of which are constantly making demands. The management of these complex demands is a major part of the organization's activities.

# ● THE LEARNING ORGANIZATION

If the characteristics of organizational health are considered worth attaining, then how can organizations go about becoming healthy and effective? An obvious way is via a cycle of learning such as that of Kolb (Kolb, Rubin, & MacIntyre, 1984):

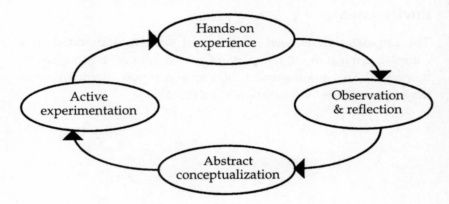

Although this cycle appears more immediately relevant to individuals than to organizations, it is nonetheless just as applicable. According to Kolb, learning is only possible if there is movement through the four steps, irrespective of where this starts.

The learning cycle describes the process whereby any organization's **capabilities** (or behavioural skills) are increased and its capacity (or potential) enhanced. It includes training and development, where **training** involves increasing particular capabilities (usually through imparting known solutions to known problems) and **development** means raising the overall level of an organization's potential.

Different levels of capability and capacity have been identified in organizations (Harrison & Robertson, 1985). These range from routine and repair capabilities for maintenance and problem-solving, respectively, through anticipatory strategic capacities, to the highest-order capacity of "**Self**-Renewal" derived from a conscious model of self-managed development (see Figure 2.3).

**FIGURE 2.3    Miles' model of managerial levels**

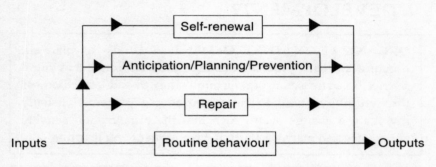

[in Harrison & Robertson, 1985]

The reference to "self" is critical. As illustrated below, it is the self-directed, insightful form of organizational learning which is most highly correlated with the effective, healthy, learning, and **developing** organization.

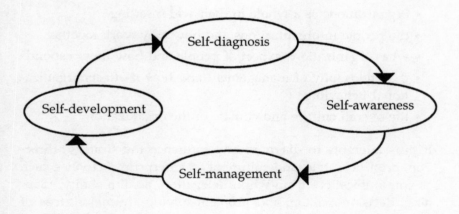

Which is where Organization **Development** comes in . . .

# • WHAT IS ORGANIZATION DEVELOPMENT?

---

**ORGANIZATION DEVELOPMENT** (OD) is a planned, organization-wide **process of change**, derived from behavioural science, to increase an organization's **health** and **effectiveness** through interventions in the organization's **processes**, usually involving a change agent, such that the organization actively anticipates and manages its own **development** and **learning**

---

**THE OBJECTIVE OF OD** is to **integrate** more fully the needs of **individuals** with the purpose or mission of their organization, such that there is better **utilization** of **resources**, notably human resources, and a consequent synergy of effort

---

OD is therefore concerned with:

- organizations as a whole in their wider setting
- the people in organizations and how they work together
- what organizations expect of people and how they respond
- the philosophy of management and how it affects organizational behaviour
- the overall culture and climate of the organization.

It thus attempts to diagnose and influence the strategy, direction, priorities, style, and culture of an enterprise. Activities such as communication, team-work, delegation, accountability, planning, decision-making, and problem-solving are major areas of interest because of their potential impact on how the organization goes about its business.

Nonetheless, it is worth noting that OD is not a technology for facilitating the imposition of specific organizational changes per se, but rather a change process for helping to establish the particular culture, behaviours, and relationships needed in a given set of circumstances.

Clearly there are some assumptions, both explicit and implicit, that are inherent in OD. They include the following:

- **Human resources** are the most important assets an organization has, and their effective management is crucial to the organization's survival and success.

- This success is most likely if the organization's **policies and procedures** are closely linked with the achievement of corporate objectives and strategic plans.

- **The organization's culture** and the values, climate, and managerial behaviour associated with that culture will exert a major influence on its achievement of excellence. This culture must therefore be managed, which means that organizational values may need to be changed or reinforced.

# ● OD INTERVENTIONS

"OD interventions are sets of structured activities whereby groups or individuals engage in tasks whose goals are organisational improvement."

[Chell, 1993]

There are various ways of categorizing OD interventions. The most comprehensive, yet concise, is that of Schmuck and Miles (1976), which covers the diagnosed problem, the mode of intervention, and the focus of that intervention (see Figure 2.4).

As can be seen in Figure 2.4, the **diagnosed problems** encompass the ways in which the organization goes about its business; the **mode** describes various methods of correction; while the **focus** can range from a holistic, whole-organizational focus through to the intrapersonal.

## FIGURE 2.4 The OD cube:
## a scheme for classifying OD interventions

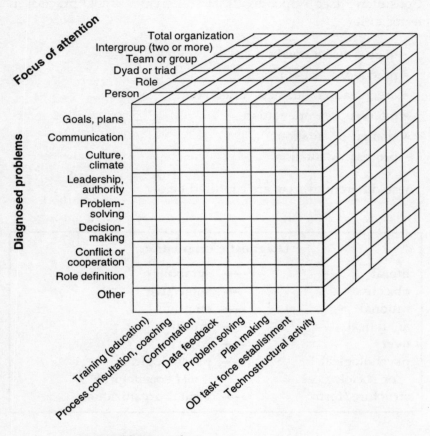

**Mode of intervention**

[from Schmuck & Miles, 1976]

An alternative but complementary approach to viewing OD interventions has been developed by Simon Vaughan, of Aspire Consultants (see Appendix 2). He differentiates OD practice in terms of its

- diagnostic orientation
- practitioner orientation
- organization/business orientation
- intervention orientation
- change orientation
- process orientation.

These different aspects are captured below.

---

### Diagnostic orientation

| literal | $\longrightarrow$ | symbolic |
| objective | $\longrightarrow$ | subjective |
| rational | $\longrightarrow$ | emotive |
| analytical | $\longrightarrow$ | intuitive |
| overt | $\longrightarrow$ | covert |
| psychological<br>  or sociological | $\longrightarrow$ | psychological<br>  *and* sociological |
| structure/form | $\longrightarrow$ | virtual organization |

---

### Practitioner orientation

| lone | $\longrightarrow$ | groups and teams |
| singular speciality | $\longrightarrow$ | multiple specialities |
| dependent<br>  or independent | $\longrightarrow$ | interdependent |
| inside or outside | $\longrightarrow$ | inside *and* outside |
| internal or external | $\longrightarrow$ | internal *and* external |
| expert/facilitator | $\longrightarrow$ | learner/developer |

## Organizational/business orientation

| | | |
|---|---|---|
| business process management | ⟶ | learning organization |
| employees, customers, suppliers | ⟶ | partners |
| shareholders | ⟶ | stakeholders |
| management | ⟶ | leadership |
| tasks | ⟶ | relationships |
| competition | ⟶ | cooperation |
| jobs | ⟶ | portfolio careers/lives |
| employment contracts | ⟶ | output contracts |
| occupational security | ⟶ | psychological security |
| programme evaluation | ⟶ | business benefits |
| hierarchical structure | ⟶ | networks |
| loyalty | ⟶ | commitment |
| rules and sanctions | ⟶ | vision and principles |
| linear thinking | ⟶ | systems thinking |
| standardization | ⟶ | diversity |
| ethical policies | ⟶ | moral actions |
| organizations as machines | ⟶ | organizations as organisms |

## Interventions orientation

| | | |
|---|---|---|
| top down/bottom up | ⟶ | inside out/outside in |
| strategy | ⟶ | implementation |
| expert design | ⟶ | co-creation |
| hierarchy and power | ⟶ | relationships and inclusion |
| silos | ⟶ | ponds |
| interpersonal and small groups | ⟶ | intrapersonal and large groups |
| emphasis on people | ⟶ | emphasis on all |
| segmented | ⟶ | integrated |
| long-term change | ⟶ | on-going change |
| remedial | ⟶ | preventative |

### Change orientation

incremental            ⟶   transformational
discontinuous         ⟶   continuous
linear                   ⟶   cyclical
creating disequilibrium   ⟶   creating balance and harmony
planning             ⟶   aligning
start/stop           ⟶   flow
single client         ⟶   multiple clients

### Process orientation

communication      ⟶   dialogue
values                   ⟶   meaning
either/or            ⟶   both/and
empowerment        ⟶   participative democracy
form                     ⟶   spirit
existing              ⟶   being
unconscious deeds    ⟶   conscious thoughts
                                         and actions

CHAPTER 3

# CONSULTING TO ORGANIZATIONS

Continuum of consultancy styles

Process consultancy roles

Theoretical approaches

Organizational context & consultant legitimacy

Consultant independence

Sources of consultants/change agents

Knowledge base & skills

Organization development can be facilitated by a change agent, who could be internal or external to the organization and whose job title could be manager, human resources professional, or consultant. In practice, a change agent operates as a **consultant** to the organization and needs the knowledge, skills, and attitudes appropriate to the consultancy role. We are defining consultancy here as **a process involving a consultant who is invited to help a client with a felt need or concern. The client can be an individual, group, or organization.** This chapter sets out the main ways consultants take up the role and describes some of the key organizational issues that must be addressed as part of that process.

# • CONTINUUM
# OF CONSULTANCY STYLES

Much OD work involves the use of individuals operating as change agents or consultants. However, consultancy means different things to different people, as expressed in the continuum of consultancy styles:

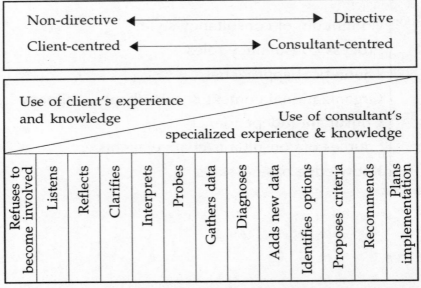

[developed in 1970 at ICI by W. H. Schmidt and A. V. Johnston]

On the left-hand side of the continuum, the consultant is client-focused, working in a process consultancy style. The consultant is listening and reflecting back on the client's issues as they are related, attempting to create an environment in which the client will come up with his/her own solutions to the problem, which can then be implemented by the client, often in collaboration with the consultant. This facilitative style can be applied to working with individuals or groups within organizations.

Further along the continuum, the consultant is adding to the process by using specific structured methods and tools of investigation, but this could still take place in a collaborative fashion with a client focus.

However, the consultant working exclusively to the right of the continuum is functioning as an expert consultant—i.e. the work is focused on the consultant's specialized experience and knowledge, and the solutions offered by the consultant are subsequently applied to the specific situation of the client. The responsibility for the creation and implementation of these solutions then lies with the consultant, rather than with the client.

Another way of understanding these differences in consultancy styles is described by Schein (1969), as set out below.

1.  **The Purchase/Expert model**

    This is the most common form of consultancy, in which a client buys expert services or information. Such a model is content-orientated and is most successful if:

    - the client has correctly diagnosed the problem
    - the client has correctly matched the available specialized expertise with the "problem" to be "solved"
    - the client has thought through the consequences of posing the "problem" and having it "solved".

    EXAMPLE

    A service manager from the product development department of a large company is very concerned about high absenteeism amongst her present VDU operators, as well as about the fact that they do not stay long in product development but ask for early transfer to other parts of the company, especially marketing. The manager wants to recruit staff who will stay within her department for a reasonable period of time. She forms the opinion that staff selection is at fault and that the time has come to do something about it. She asks an organizational development consultant to come up with a questionnaire to help in the selection of VDU operators.

2. **The Doctor–Patient model**

Here, the clients are aware of some "symptoms" of their problems—e.g. "Our staff morale is very low"—but they have not come up with any diagnosis. They expect the consultant to pinpoint the cause of any problems and prescribe remedies. It is most successful if:

- the client has correctly interpreted the "symptoms"
- the consultant correctly diagnoses the problem and prescribes appropriate solutions
- the client accepts the prescription and will do what the consultant recommends.

EXAMPLE

The same service manager from the product development department asks an OD consultant to help her with the problem with the VDU operators.

The consultant investigates the causes of the absenteeism and high staff turnover by meeting the staff individually. He diagnoses a high level of stress and burnout amongst the VDU operators. He offers to organize a stress management workshop for all the staff of the department, including the VDU operators.

3. **The Process Consultancy model**

In this model, the consultant is less concerned with the content of a problem, and more with the **process** by which the individual, group, or organization identifies and solves problems. The model focuses on helping clients form their own diagnoses on the basis of their proximity to and understanding of the associated issues. Clients are then helped to generate, select, and implement any associated solutions. It is based on the following assumptions:

- the client seeks help when he/she does not know exactly what the problem is

- the client does not know what help is available or relevant to the problem
- the client benefits from participation in the diagnostic process
- the client knows what interventions will work
- the client benefits from learning how to solve problems him/herself.

EXAMPLE

The same service manager from the product development department asks an OD consultant to help her with this problem of high absenteeism and turnover in VDU operators.

The consultant decides to investigate the problem by holding a series of exploratory meetings with the manager and the VDU operators. During these meetings, the poor working conditions of the operators are noted—that they work in isolated and poorly lit and ventilated cubicles, and that their break times are staggered so they can never meet one another or other members of staff. This leads to a sense of alienation, isolation, and high levels of stress. Furthermore, the operators do not have a clear picture of the whole enterprise and their contribution to it. It is thought likely that other professional groups in the department feel the same and that the sense of wholeness of the work is felt only by the manager.

In the light of these conclusions, it is agreed to hold a series of department development seminars for all the staff to explore their understanding of and connection to the enterprise of the department—and subsequently how best to organize and improve the working environment for all staff members to facilitate their collaborative effort.

Schein suggests that consultants should always **start in the process consultancy mode**, so that clients continue to own their own problems, even if, later on, it becomes appropriate to offer expert solutions. In this way, the client concerns are seen in a broader context and the effort to address them becomes a shared enterprise more likely to be owned by the organization as a whole and thus more effective.

"Thus the primary though not the exclusive function of OD consultants is to help clients learn how to help themselves more effectively. Although consultants occasionally provide expert information [Purchase/Expert Model] and may some-times prescribe a remedy [Doctor–Patient Model], their more typical mode of operating is facilitating."

[Burke, 1987, p. 145]

# ● PROCESS CONSULTANCY ROLES

Within the process consultancy model there are several different roles available to the consultant or change agent (these terms are used interchangeably from now on), as described in Table 3.1.

### TABLE 3.1 Consulting—the associated skills

| Roles | Activities | Results |
| --- | --- | --- |
| Diagnoser | Obtaining facts and analysing them | Data about key issues for more effective decision-making. |
| Planner | Helping set up action plans and developing strategy | Data priorities. Actions proposed to solve issues suggested by the data/situation. Plans to move proposals into action. |
| Assistant problem solver | Helping the client to clarify and analyse the problem and develop an action plan to handle the problem | Problems identified and defined. Forces affecting the problem analysed. Action steps developed for managing the problem/opportunity. |
| Team builder | Providing teams with ways to increase their effectiveness | Greater team capacity for open communication and data flow. Improved work group problem-solving and decision-making. Increased common knowledge and skills. Improved work climate. |
| Conflict manager | Helping to examine and reduce conflict situations where feasible | Conflict handled creatively. Reduction of conflict where appropriate. |
| Systems analyst | Examining how such areas as structure, decision-making communications, personnel procedures, rewards/punishments, and employee participation affect the functioning of an organization | An analysis of how effective an organizational system is in the way it is formed and functioning. |

(*continued*)

**TABLE 3.1   Consulting—the associated skills** (*continued*)

| Roles | Activities | Results |
| --- | --- | --- |
| Process observer | Viewing and analysing an individual's or work group's functioning | An analysis of what is working well, what needs improving—how work gets done, how communication takes place, how problem-solving/decision-making is utilized, and how an effective work climate is maintained |
| Change process expert | Giving input/methodologies on the impact of change and how to plan for it | A review of effect of change on individual work group and on organizational functioning and productivity. Planned change, rather than haphazard reactions to problems/opportunities. Ways to meet resistance to change. |
| Individual developer | Helping individual managers to analyse, problem solve; helping to develop career paths | Special attention given to key issues and to management needs. Persons with increased sense of a career path and with action plans to bring about their career directions. |
| Organization developer | Assisting work groups, individuals, and organizations in bringing about planned change | A focused, planned effort to increase effectiveness within an organization or amongst its employees and work groups. |
| Interpersonal developer | Providing ways to enrich human interaction and enhance working relationships and climate | More effective communication and interpersonal relationships. An improved work climate. |
| Skills builder | Providing training for individual work group and organizational growth—using a variety of methods | Persons with new or enhanced skills in such areas as interpersonal relationships, management leadership, problem-solving/decision-making, group effectiveness, communications, motivation, creativity. |

[prepared for the Effectiveness Resource Group in 1974 by D. Swartz and J. Faban]

# ● THEORETICAL APPROACHES

There are a number of theoretical approaches that can be identified. These are listed below, together with brief descriptions and suggestions for further reading.

1. **Systems approaches**

   a. **Open systems approach**

   This approach focuses on the dynamic relationship between the organization and its environment, exploring the transformational processes and structures by which an organization achieves its primary task. It assumes that the survival of the organization depends on managing the boundary with the external world, in terms of inputs and outputs.

   (Miller & Rice, 1967; Morgan, 1986)

   b. **"Recursive systems" approach**

   This approach focuses on thinking of organizations as multi-layered systems or patterns of interaction between individuals or groups, which can become confused and dysfunctional. If the feedback loops between individuals and groups can be explored, more effective strategies for accomplishing the task of the organization can be generated.

   (Campbell, Draper, & Huffington, 1991; Cronen & Pearce, 1980; McCaughan & Palmer, 1994; Watzlawick, Weakland, & Fisch, 1974)

2. **Psychoanalytic approach**

   This approach focuses on deep psychological processes in groups and organizations which create barriers to solving organizational problems and which, if addressed, can release creativity and original solutions. This approach focuses on the dynamics of working groups, or group relations.

   (De Board, 1978; Hirschhorn, 1988; Obholzer & Roberts, 1994)

### 3.  Behavioural approach

This approach focuses on the behaviour exhibited by individuals, groups, or organizations, and it attempts to describe, explain, predict, and, where possible, manage them on the basis of a behavioural psychology. That is, behaviour is primarily learned and then maintained by contingencies operating in the environment. Such behaviour can be healthy and constructive but can equally be deemed dysfunctional or pathological, depending on the consequences it obtains.

(Chell, 1993)

In practice, these approaches are often combined to create an effective intervention.

# ● ORGANIZATIONAL CONTEXT & CONSULTANT LEGITIMACY

An important distinction is whether consultants are internal or external to the organization in question, and whether their role is legitimate (i.e. organizationally sanctioned) or otherwise:

**Consultant legitimacy:**
**internal or external to the organization**

|  | Internal | External |
|---|---|---|
| **Legitimate** | Internal change agent formally recognized by the organization, e.g. management development advisors, human resources personnel, internal consultancy department | External consultant brought in on a formal contract by the organization |
| **Not legitimate** | Covert change agent working as a "mole" | "Agent provocateur" not formally recognized by the organization but usually working overtly, e.g. political pressure groups, private advisors to management, "old boy" networks |

Consultants who find themselves working without organizational sanction within their own or client organizations will find that their effectiveness is severely limited and their efforts will probably fail.

Some of the conditions that need to be in place within the consultant's own organization and in the client organization to provide the basis for legitimate and effective work are set out below:

### Consultant legitimacy:
### own organization and client organization

|  | Own organization | Client organization |
| --- | --- | --- |
| **Legitimate** | Sanctioned by manager<br>Rewards commensurate with consultancy practice<br>Support, supervision, and training<br>Job title reflecting wider role | Consultancy services explicitly requested<br>Open or flexible initial brief<br>Closed brief but capable of renegotiation |
| **Not legitimate** | Not sanctioned by manager<br>Rewards for other activities<br>Lack of support, etc.<br>Job title describing different role<br>Secret or covert activity of questionable status | Consultancy services not requested explicitly or closed brief<br>Possible low opinion of consultants |

A further aspect of one's ability to function effectively as a consultant is the degree of independent action possible within one's own and in the client organization. Some of the conditions that need to be in place are set out in the next section, on independence.

# ● CONSULTANT INDEPENDENCE

| | |
|---|---|
| **Independent** | Able to make decisions, give advice without reference to superior/manager |
| | Able to engage in a dialogue with client— responsibility for outcome is shared |
| | Able to recommend courses of action/product regardless of benefit to own organization |
| | Able to draw on examples of practice in a variety of similar and different organizations |
| **Not independent** | Unable to operate without sanction from manager |
| | Power relationship with client is skewed in such a way that open dialogue is difficult/ impossible |
| | Unable to recommend any course of action not of direct benefit to own organization |
| | Not able to draw on other experience, because restricted to this client organization |
| | Too close to client issues to draw back and offer a different view |
| | Conflicts of interest/loyalties |

# • SOURCES OF CONSULTANTS/ CHANGE AGENTS

There are three principle sources:

1. Managers responsible for developing their own departments, directorates, or organizations.
2. Those individuals specializing in OD as a profession.
3. Those professionals in a field allied to OD, such as human resources, job evaluation, management training and development, and many others.

# ● KNOWLEDGE BASE & SKILLS

There are several "checklists" available, but in essence these comprise the following:

**OD theory**

> e.g.   a general knowledge of planned change and action research

**Intrapersonal skills**

> e.g.   conceptual analysis
>
> integrity
>
> entrepreneurial skills
>
> personal stress management

**Interpersonal skills**

> e.g.   listening
>
> establishing rapport
>
> counselling and coaching

**Technical skills**

> e.g.   data-collection
>
> organizational analysis
>
> designing and implementing interventions (see chapter 5)

**Integrative consulting skills**

While intrapersonal, interpersonal, and technical skills are relevant to the content, process, and context of an organizational change, there is also a higher order of integrative skills. These encompass the overall management of any consultancy process, both operationally and strategically, as well as the integration of different developmental stages and levels of intervention into a synergistic whole.

The effective consultant blends the above knowledge and skills into the following:

---

**CONSULTANCY ABILITIES**

1. to tolerate ambiguity

2. to influence

3. to confront difficult issues

4. to support and comfort others

5. to listen well and empathize

6. to recognize one's own feelings and intuitions quickly

7. to conceptualize

8. to discover and mobilize human energy

9. to teach or create learning opportunities

10. to maintain a sense of humour!

---

[after Burke, 1987]

# CHAPTER 4

# EXTERNAL AND INTERNAL CONSULTANCY

# ● DEFINITIONS

**External Consultancy** involves consultancy to individuals, groups, or organizations *outside* the organization of which the Consultant is a member or employee.

**Internal Consultancy** involves consultancy to individuals, groups, or the whole organization of which the Consultant is also a member or employee.

# ● INCREASING RELEVANCE OF INTERNAL CONSULTANCY

The need for consultancy within one's own organization, even if not formally requested, is becoming increasingly relevant. This is because of the need for organizations to work through the constant cultural and structural changes they are facing. Internal consultancy may also be an integral part of the work of many professionals who may not have the word "consultant" in their job title.

# ● APPROPRIATE TASKS FOR INTERNAL AND EXTERNAL CONSULTANTS

EXTERNAL CONSULTANCY IS APPROPRIATE WHEN
THERE IS A NEED:

- to introduce a major organizational change, particularly when consultation with the Board is necessary or the organization does not have the expertise required—e.g. business process management, quality, risk assessment
- for an outside perspective on the organization
- for a consultant who does not have a conflict of interest or loyalty, nor an axe to grind.

INTERNAL CONSULTANCY IS APPROPRIATE WHEN
THERE IS A NEED TO:

- work with the consequences of organizational change
- rely on skills accessed and built from within the organization
- develop good knowledge of local issues and resources
- facilitate growth of a broad base of support for change
- own the change effort and for continuing presence throughout implementation, especially when this is anticipated to take years rather than months.

[adapted from Basset & Brunning, 1994]

# ● THE CHALLENGES FOR INTERNAL CONSULTANTS

Individuals are increasingly requested to take the role of consultant or trouble-shooter from within the organization. Although this is a legitimate and a recognized position, the role of internal consultant can be complex.

- **Internal consultants' views of problems will inevitably be affected by the beliefs about the process of change that brought their role into being in the first place.**

  For example views about how the organization should change, at what rate, through which channels, supporting which relationships, etc. This can make it difficult for the internal consultant to develop an independent view of the situation.

- **Other people in the organization may interpret the intervention of internal consultants as biased in some way.**

  That is, others will assume that the internal consultant was brought in to support the positions and policies of those who requested help in the first place. Those being consulted will have views about the gains and losses associated with changes in the organization. These views are expressed through the belief system or culture of the organization, which in turn organizes various roles and relationships.

  Those listening to the internal consultant will ask themselves, "Whose side is this person on?" "Are his/her views acceptable to my manager and the higher levels of the organization?" "What will happen to me if I go along with the consultant—and what if I don't?" When people begin asking these questions, the position of the internal consultant shifts into a larger context, which includes behaviours and relationships beyond the immediate and apparent relationship between internal consultants and their internal clients who are also colleagues.

- **The stages of consulting cannot be so neatly defined and concluded for internal consultants,** who remain a part of the organization to which they are consulting, potentially constrained by all the positive and negative effects of their interventions and their inability to leave the system.

(For further reading, see Huffington & Brunning, 1994.)

# CHAPTER 5

# THE CONSULTANCY PROCESS

Key stages in OD consulting

Scouting

Entry

Contracting

Data-gathering

Diagnosis

Planning

Intervention

Evaluation

Withdrawal

# ● KEY STAGES IN OD CONSULTING

**1.    Scouting**

Change agent decides whether or not to "enter" system

**2.    Entry**

Establishing a relationship with the client as a basis for further involvement

**3.    Contracting**

Developing a mutual contract, clarifying expectations and *modus operandi*

**4.    Data-gathering**

Measuring organizational indices and variables

**5.    Diagnosis**

Interpreting the data, feeding it back to the client, and developing a joint understanding

**6.    Planning**

Identifying specific interventions, including who will do what, and how it might be evaluated

**7.    Intervention**

Carrying out the planned implementations

**8.    Evaluation**

Assessing the success of the interventions and the need for further action or withdrawal

**9.    Withdrawal**

If no further action by the change agent is required, managing the termination of the OD work, while at the same time leaving the system with an enhanced capacity to manage change by itself, in the future

Most OD work involves the use of some kind of change agent, internal or external, to the organization and "legitimized" or otherwise. The role of change agent at each stage of the consultancy process is explored more fully in the next sections.

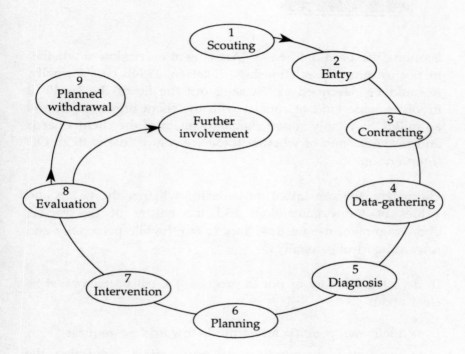

## ● SCOUTING

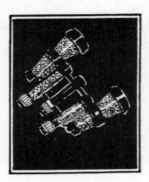

Scouting has been defined as "Arriving at a decision of whether or not to pursue a relationship" (Nielsen, 1984). Less formally, it could be described as "sussing out the lie of the land". It involves some kind of contact with the client organization and an initial, inevitably superficial, assessment of the client's needs and resources and of whether these are compatible with an OD intervention.

Ultimately, the consultant must decide whether the vision and values of the organization, and the nature of the project and assignment in question, appear worthwhile personally and rewarding professionally.

In deciding whether or not to proceed, the consultants must be clear about:

- their own position and attitude towards the request
- the issues surrounding the organization requesting the project
- the issues surrounding the actual nature of the project.

A further dimension to the role of change agents is whether they operate as "conformist" or "deviant" innovators (Legge, 1978):

"Conformist" innovators endeavour to relate their activities to organizationally defined success criteria, rather than attempting to alter the organization. They associate themselves with the organization's values and behaviour. They accept the organization for what it is, so that their role is primarily one of enhancing the organization's effectiveness by improving the quality of managerial efforts.

"Deviant" innovators, however, do try to influence dominant organizational values, notably where these are not necessarily the same as society's. They aim to use more "humanistic" values as a reference point for the organization and hope to affect the organization's values and behaviour in this direction.

The following questions (adapted from Basset & Brunning, 1994, and Broome, 1995) may help the prospective consultant decide whether to accept or decline a request.

## ABOUT THE REQUEST ITSELF

- Who is the client?
- Who is the sponsor (i.e. the champion of the work, who may not be directly involved but whose support is essential)?
- What is being asked of the consultant?
- What is the real issue at stake?
- Is there a difference between what the consultant is expected to do and the real issue(s)?
- Can the real issue be worked with/addressed?

## ABOUT THE CLIENT ORGANIZATION
## MAKING THE REQUEST

- Do I as a consultant agree with the overall principles/values underpinning this organization and this particular piece of work?

- Who are the basic stakeholders in this organization? Who stands to gain/lose as a result of this project being undertaken by me?
- Will the employing organization generally be welcoming to a consultant?
- Are people/departments/parts of the organization being excluded from this piece of work when they could or perhaps should be included?
- Is this organization capable of learning/developing/using the consulting process to their advantage?
- What will change/improve/worsen in the organization as a result of this project?
- Do they really need a consultant—or could they do it better/ as well on their own?

## ABOUT THE PROJECT
## AS DEFINED BY THE CLIENT ORGANIZATION

- Is this work achievable?
- Is this an exciting piece of work?
- How much pressure will there be and from where?
- Is this project/process empowering? To whom?
- How will the piece of work finish?
- What will the end product be? Will it lead to new/other developments?
- Who will be managing my work?
- To whom will I be responsible/accountable for the project?
- Will I be given access to all levels of organization relevant to my work?
- What about the resources available from the organization?
- What are these resources, and who will approve their use?

## ABOUT YOU AS THE CONSULTANT

- How will I be supported and enabled to do the work?
- Should it really be me, or are there others who could do this project better, more easily, or more economically than I?
- Do I need this project?

If these questions can be resolved to the consultant's satisfaction, the consultant proceeds with the next stage, a more formal enquiry on a similar list of questions, namely ENTRY.

## ● ENTRY

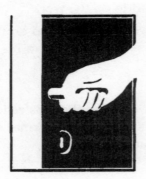

Entry is the more formal beginning of the client/consultant association. For the consultant it will be an important opportunity to gather more data in support of the initial information generated during the previous SCOUTING stage.

The formal enquiry may follow the same pattern of information-seeking as covered in ENTRY; in order to gain clarity about essential issues, consultants will be relying on their skills of:

- asking questions and probing for clarity/understanding
- being attentive to the overt and covert messages given
- understanding the client's perspective and needs
- building trust and credibility
- legitimizing the process of consultancy
- establishing their credentials
- securing agreement to work in the client's system
- assessing readiness and expectations
- testing hypotheses about the presenting problem
- testing one's own understanding of the organization and its primary preoccupations
- understanding where the organization is in relation to its own cycle of development (see Figure 5.2, p. 68).

Once there is a shared understanding between the client and the consultant that consultancy is required and desirable for the benefit of the organization, the next stage of the consulting process is entered into: the formal CONTRACTING stage.

# ● CONTRACTING

The contract is the explicit agreement between the client and the consultant regarding:

- the scope of the OD intervention
- its broad objectives
- methodology
- access to the organization and its database
- access to individuals and/or de facto clients
- the role of the consultant
- reporting relationships
- likely involvement of the client (e.g. in introductions, lobbying, etc.)
- the modus operandi or ground rules (e.g. confidentiality)
- likely time-scale and costs involved
- regular opportunities for reviews and renegotiation over time
- evaluation.

At the point of agreeing a contract with the client organization, the consultant should also be aware of the less formal but none-theless important issue of the **psychological contract**. This refers to a mutual sense of willingness to collaborate productively and is quite distinct from the legal or financial contract, expressed perhaps by "We can do business together". It is usually unwritten and unspoken, but it is critical to the subsequent success of the venture. When the psychological contract is robust, it is much easier to explore assumptions and expectations and to raise issues of autonomy and power that, if unacknowledged, can undermine the basis on which the client/consultant partnership is founded.

For fuller discussion of these issues, see Huffington and Brunning (1994).

# • DATA-GATHERING

Data collection in OD involves the **formal** gathering of information on particular organizational features, such as the inputs, transformation processes, and outputs mentioned in chapter 2.

In addition to such observations, there are a number of other more formal and objective data-gathering techniques, which could be represented as in Table 5.1.

**Informal** data-gathering will inevitably be happening from the very start of any OD contact, and more experienced consultants will be gathering such intelligence from the very beginning of their engagement with the organization.

For instance, if the consultant is always kept waiting for appointments, the meetings never start on time, or the stakeholders invited to the meetings do not turn up or come unprepared, the consultant may use this additional information in support of the formal data available.

### TABLE 5.1. Data-gathering techniques

| Techniques | Advantages | Disadvantages |
|---|---|---|
| Observations | Direct<br>Free of self-report biases<br>Insightful<br>Augments other methods of data collection | Observer must be skilled and unbiased |
| Interviews | More personalized<br>Provide opportunity to clarify aims of exercise<br>Can cover previously unanticipated issues<br>Facilitate 1:1 and 1:group relationships<br>Structured or semi-structured or unstructured<br>Can be modified<br>Enable probing of issues | Time-consuming<br>Risk of self-report bias<br>Requires a skilled interviewer<br>Risk of interviewer bias |
| Questionnaires | Cheaper than interviewing<br>Efficient<br>Can be computerized<br>Can be standardized<br>Can be customized<br>Useful if organization is large<br>Provide quantitative information<br>Can be built up from interview data | Limited qualitative information<br>Impersonal<br>Risk of response bias<br>Risk of insensitive administration<br>Possible poor design |
| Organizational records e.g. company records archives complaints written policies etc. | Useful source of data on "structural" components e.g. jobs, reward systems, turnover, absenteeism, etc.<br>More objective<br>Free from respondent bias<br>Quantifiable | Incomplete data<br>Built-in bias<br>Not always easily accessible<br>Often commercially sensitive |

# ● DIAGNOSIS

After the data-gathering stage, effective diagnosis is required if subsequent OD interventions are to be successful. In OD terms, it does not refer to a narrow medical definition; rather, it is a collaborative effort, usually involving the consultant in feeding back data to the client, followed by a joint effort at drawing conclusions to inform any future action plan.

Any data fed back to the client organization for use in joint diagnosis should ideally meet certain criteria:

---

**Ideal Characteristics of Feedback Data**

- meaningful
- comprehensible
- descriptive
- verifiable
- not overwhelming
- impactful
- comparative—explained in context
- unfinalized—not seen as a one-off exercise

---

[Mohrman, Cummings, & Lawler, 1983]

Diagnosis is usually derived from the conceptual model of how organizations function (see Figure 2.1). Another model, developed by International Training Services (ITS: see Appendix 2), is "The Organizational Wheel", as shown in Figure 5.1.

According to ITS, the individual parts of the wheel and the hub are interrelated. By using data generated under each of the wheel's parts, the "wheel" analysis provides:

- causal links between any problems
- information on the principal factors for change
- identification of the organization's learning needs and opportunities.

FIGURE 5.1   The organizational wheel

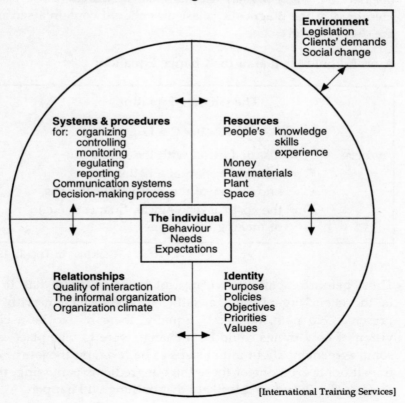

[International Training Services]

# ● PLANNING

Depending on the data gathered, the diagnosis reached, and the interventions available, a process of specific actions can be decided on. Such a plan should ideally address those issues identified in the diagnostic phase and should contain a sense of the desired future state.

A useful guide is that of the Change Equation:

---

**The Change Equation**

$$A \times B \times C > D$$

where    A = dissatisfaction with the status quo
                 B = a shared vision of a better future
                 C = knowledge of the first practical steps
                 D = the cost (psychological, financial, etc.)
                       of making the change

---

[Gleicher, in Turrill, 1986]

Thus, before embarking on any intervention, there has to be in the client organization a sufficient dissatisfaction with the present: "No pain, no gain!" Equally, there has to be a clear vision of how things could be if change were to take place, and some agreement about initial steps to be taken on the journey of transition. If even one of these three ingredients is missing, then $A \times B \times C = 0$, and so it is likely that nothing will happen.

# ● INTERVENTION

According to Burke (1987) , an OD intervention encompasses:

> ". . . some specific activity, some event, or planned sequence
> of events, that occur as a result of diagnosis and feedback . . .
> provided the event 1) responds to an actual and felt need for
> change on the part of the client, 2) involves the client in the
> planning and implementing of the change, and 3) leads to
> change in the organisation's culture."
>
> [p. 112]

One way of representing the range of interventions in addition
to Figure 2.4 (the OD cube) is given overleaf in Table 5.2.

Consultants may be helped in their attempts to clarify issues
and select the most appropriate interventions by considering the
organization's stage in its life-cycle (see Figure 5.2). This model
can apply to a whole organization or to teams, subgroups, or
units within an organization.

**TABLE 5.2**

| Depth & nature of intervention | System level | Task issues |
|---|---|---|
| ORGANIZATIONAL ⬆ | **1. The whole organization** | Strategic thinking, strategy development, planning transitions and change; management of the boundaries with the wider system; organizational design; diagnosing organizational effectiveness, designing and initiating processes to improve it. |
| | **2. Inter-group** | Managing the interfaces between all major functions/parts of the organization; work flow; meshing of roles and responsibilities; identifying blocks and helping forces, and planning action on them. |
| | **3. Team** | Goal-setting and clarity. Congruence with mission. Derivation of performance criteria. Role definition and clarity of responsibilities. Effective meetings. |
| THERAPEUTIC | **4. Inter-personal** | Role definition and negotiation. Boss/subordinate issues, e.g. delegation, accountability, freedom to act; performance review and feedback. |
| ⬇ | **5. Individual** | Foil for testing thinking, sounding board. Role definition and clarification. Meetings preparation; action planning. |

## Aspects of organization development interventions

| Process issues | The clients at this system level |
|---|---|
| Visioning, developing organisational identity, building commitment; representing and marketing the organisation to the wider system/outside world; diagnosing and managing organizational condition, climate and culture; building the organization as a learning system; raising organizational capacity. | Top managers and top management teams. |
| Articulating inter-group perspectives, inter-group conflict resolution. | Heads of functions/departmental fuctional/departmental management teams. |
| Team-building. Commitment. Group dynamics facilitation. | Teams at any organisational level. |
| Interpersonal relationships. Interpersonal conflict resolution. Managerial counselling, subordinate development. Role negotiation. | Pairs of individuals, or their managers, at any organizational level. |
| Assistance with professional and personal review, e.g. management style and values, life goals, job and personal transitions; skills development, individual learning, individual visioning. | Individuals at any organizational level. |

[Reproduced with the kind permission of Shell UK's OD unit]

**FIGURE 5.2   The organizational life-cycle**

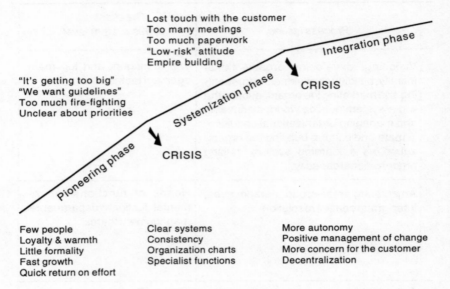

Lost touch with the customer
Too many meetings
Too much paperwork
"Low-risk" attitude
Empire building

Integration phase

"It's getting too big"
"We want guidelines"
Too much fire-fighting
Unclear about priorities

CRISIS

Systemization phase

CRISIS

Pioneering phase

| Few people | Clear systems | More autonomy |
| Loyalty & warmth | Consistency | Positive management of change |
| Little formality | Organization charts | More concern for the customer |
| Fast growth | Specialist functions | Decentralization |
| Quick return on effort | | |

[from work done in 1988 by Valerie Stewart of British Rail]

The stages of Pioneering, Systematization, and Integration in Figure 5.2 give rise to different types of developmental "crisis"; the symptoms of these crises are shown above the developmental line. If these crises are to be resolved, interventions in the directions shown below the line are appropriate at each point. If one imagines the model applying to a large unit or whole organization, one can visualize a new organization growing fast but reaching a point where it needs to become less focused on a charismatic leader and more on systems and routines for working effectively. Further down the line, these systems could become rigid and bureaucratic and might interfere with growth and development. The organizations may then need to divide into further autonomous specialist units to continue to thrive. Then each of these units could be considered to be at the pioneering stage again, thus completing the cycle.

# ● EVALUATION

"Does OD work? . . . In general the answer is 'YES, OD can have positive effects on individuals, work groups and organisations in terms of attitude changes, behaviour changes and performance changes'. Evaluating OD programs is a complicated and difficult undertaking, however. . . ."

[French & Bell, 1978]

The first issue, of course, is whether evaluation is conducted for curiosity-based outcome research or for knowledge generation to aid the consultancy process itself. If the former, then there are numerous problems with carefully controlled OD research, notably in demonstrating any causal link between the OD intervention or "treatment" and its dependent variables (see French & Bell, 1978, for discussion).

Outcome measures and audit of the consultative process should really be agreed at the contracting stage, so that the client and the consultant, as well as other important stakeholders, will be in a position at the end of the process of consultancy to check whether the agreed process/outcome/results/changes etc. have been reached and with what effect.

Countless case studies of effective organizational change do exist, and this is evidenced in a mushrooming of associated literature.

What has emerged from work to date is an appreciation of those factors correlated with successful OD.

---

### Factors associated with successful OD

- awareness by key people of organizational problems
- appreciation by key people of the contribution of OD
- the introduction into the system of a behavioural scientist as change agent
- support from the top of the organization
- comprehensive diagnosis
- early successes
- open educational philosophy about OD
- development of internal OD resources
- effective management of the OD process

---

Some of the case studies provide important lessons in relation to which interventions were effective and which were not, and which organizational circumstances were more conducive to a successful intervention.

Finally, as with the choice of appropriate intervention, the evaluation should not be too mechanical a process, but one that allows a joint reflection on other relevant achievements of the project such as: new developments and possibilities, fresh perceptions and capabilities, and, most importantly, new learning.

# ● WITHDRAWAL

Managing disengagement from any intervention is a skilled task. Above all, it is a matter of timing and of judgement. Clients will hopefully consider that they have a satisfactory outcome, and that any resultant changes can be maintained in the client system.

Consultants must also judge whether responsibility and owner-ship for the work is secure enough for the clients to be able to manage similar changes in the future. Only then is it timely to negotiate an ending of the consultancy relationship or to agree whether further intervention is appropriate. If the latter applies, then a new process of consultancy can begin.

However, in the spirit of process consultancy, it must be ac-knowledged that the organization may have changed as a result of the consultant's work, and so too has the consultant by being part of that process. So it could be that new opportunities for creative consultancy work present themselves in this ending process and that sometimes it would be inappropriate to exit the system too finally.

For those who work as internal consultants, the formal ending of a given project and associated "de-roling" can be a difficult process. If not executed with clarity, then there may be role confusion and a lingering sense of responsibility on the part of the consultant.

Examples of ways in which consultants can signal both concretely and symbolically the end of their involvement with a given project include:

- a written report
- a formal presentation
- a formal action plan
- a celebration of success.

# CHAPTER 6

# CHANGE MANAGEMENT

Content of change
Some assumptions
Some guidelines for successful change efforts
Some observations on successful change efforts
Personal ground rules for change agents

# ● CONTENT OF CHANGE

How do organizations typically go about defining the content of their change?

- **Assessment of internal and external environment**

  First of all, in order to change, an organization requires an appraisal of its internal and external environment. Analysing threats and opportunities, strengths and weaknesses, resources and opportunities is the cornerstone of strategic management.

- **Strategic options**

  From this assessment, strategic options will be formulated. These can range from doing the same thing to distinctly different ways of doing things, as illustrated in Figure 6.1.

- **Strategic intent**

  In order to change, however, there needs to be a well-defined strategic intent—i.e. the new direction, the new purpose, of the organization. This will constitute the input of the change process, which will in turn lead to a modification of that strategic process in an interactive fashion.

### FIGURE 6.1  Marketing activities

|  | Existing product/ service/activity | New product/ service/activity |
|---|---|---|
| **Existing market** | Maintaining/increasing market share | New product development |
| **New market** | New market development | Diversification |

- **Future present**

  Strategic intent creates a future, a vision of a better world, and change is about trading the present for the future.

In undertaking a planned process of change, certain assumptions and values are either explicit, or more usually implicit, in the process. The remainder of this chapter is a distillation of ideas predominantly from the work of Richard Beckhard (Beckhard & Harris, 1987), which attempts to capture those essential assumptions and to offer some practical and personal guidelines.

# ● SOME ASSUMPTIONS

**Individuals:**

- want to grow and develop
- want their organization to succeed
- tend to be resistant to change, particularly if goals or means towards it are unclear
- can learn to analyse a situation and plan its change
- tend to support change more if involved in its planning
- have membership in several groups—e.g. subordinate, head of a work family, colleague group, etc.—so effective work performance requires effective leadership and membership skills

**About organizations:**

- organizations are composed of overlapping work groups
- any change in a sub-system is likely to affect the whole system
- any aspect of the system—e.g. morale, communications, loyalty, effectiveness—is held in an equilibrium by opposing forces
- hierarchical organizations tend to have low openness due to low level of trust
- norms are often used for avoiding or suppressing conflict

**Change agents:**

- must establish a personal relationship of trust and confidence early on
- should deal with the dependency relationship between themselves and their client
- should concentrate on problem diagnosis
- should resist the temptation to control the situation or client
- should avoid defending, advising, persuading, or censoring
- should build in plans for stabilization and maintenance of change without dependence on them

## ● SOME GUIDELINES FOR SUCCESSFUL CHANGE EFFORTS

**Clear analysis of . . .**
- definition of the change problem:
    - — what types of change are indicated?
    - — where are the systems related to the problem?
- aims and objectives, final and interim
- methods to be used and consequences
- priorities:
    - — what is the starting point?
    - — where do you have the most leverage?

**Contracting . . .**

- obtain consensus on aims, methods, and roles
- use a joint problem-solving approach
- involve those affected by the change
- agree a clear contract that is not watered down

**Develop an Activity or Process Plan in which . . .**

- activities are clearly identified rather than broadly generalized
- activities are closely linked to change goals
- people understand exactly what their roles are
- there is a timetable of activities with deadlines and targets
- there are contingency plans
- cost effectiveness has been considered
- the involvement and support at the top is overt
- continual monitoring and review is built into the process, with agreed criteria for evaluation

**Develop a Commitment Plan in which . . .**

- target individuals whose commitment is needed are identified ("critical mass")
- the commitment of each individual in the "critical mass" is assessed
- there is a plan for obtaining necessary commitment from the "critical mass" and means for monitoring it, e.g. by:
    - problem-finding activities and educational efforts to create awareness of the problem
    - treating "hurting" systems, or those who are suffering most by things not changing
    - changing the reward system to value different behaviour
    - changing the behaviour of leaders, so that they can act as role models
    - forced collaboration mechanisms in which people are required to work together and take on certain managerial roles

# ● SOME OBSERVATIONS ON SUCCESSFUL CHANGE EFFORTS

**Conditions that must exist or be "engineered":**

- shared dissatisfaction with the status quo
- shared vision of the future and aims for change
- knowledge about "first practical steps"
- economic and psychological costs for people must not be greater than the above three points
- the organization operates in a goal-directed mode
- decision-making is based on who is close to the issue, rather than position in role or hierarchy
- reward systems are related to the work to be done
- communication is relatively open
- collaboration is rewarded
- conflict is managed, not suppressed or avoided
- the organization is seen as an open system
- individuality and individuals are valued
- an "action-research" mode of management exists, incorporating feedback systems for monitoring

# ● PERSONAL GROUND RULES FOR CHANGE AGENTS

- Prepare for change in a constructive way to minimize the effect of setbacks
- Build support, or a "scaffolding"
- Set realistic objectives
- Do not worry about obstacles
- Test on a small scale at first, if appropriate, by pilot projects
- Be positive about the potential of the change
- Keep an eye on the end product
- Do not take on too much change at any one time
- Retain a sense of control of all, or at least part of, the change
- Minimize other areas of stress and pressure in your life while undergoing change
- Accept the inevitability of change and the impossibility of achieving permanent stability

# REFERENCES

Adams, J. D., & Spencer, S. (1986).
The Strategic Leadership Perspective. In: J. Adams (Eds.),
*Transforming Leadership.* Winchester, VA: Miles River Press.

Basset, T., & Brunning, H. (1994).
The Ins and Outs of Consultancy. *The Journal of Practice and
Staff Development, 4* (1).

Beckhard, R., & Harris, R. T. (1987).
*Organisational Transitions: Managing Complex Change.* Reading. MA: Addison-Wesley.

Broome, A. (1995).
Internal Consultant: Pearl or Irritant? *Clinical Psychology in
Organisational Consultancy* (Newsletter, No. 11, Spring).

Burke, W. W. (1987).
*Organisation Development: A Normative View.* Reading, MA:
Addison-Wesley.

Campbell, D., Draper, R., & Huffington, C. (1991).
*A Systemic Approach to Consultation.* London: Karnac Books.

Chell, E. (1993).
*The Psychology of Behaviour in Organisations.* London:
Macmillan.

Cronen, V., & Pearce, W. B. (1980).
*Communication, Action and Meaning: The Creation of Social
Realities.* New York: Praeger.

De Board, R. (1978).
*Psychoanalysis of Organisation: A Psychoanalytic Approach to
Understanding Organisations.* London: Tavistock
Publications.

Fisher, D., & Torbert W. R. (1995).
*Personal and Organisational Transformations.* Maidenhead:
McGraw-Hill.

French, W., & Bell, W. H. (1978).
*Organisation Development.* Englewood Cliffs, NJ: Prentice-
Hall.

Garratt, B. (1987).
*The Learning Organisation.* London: Fontana/Collins.

Harrison, E. G., & Robertson, M. J. (1985).
O.D. An Alternative Strategy for Organisational Renewal in
the NHS? *Hospital and Health Services Review*, 125–129.

Hirschhorn, L. (1988).
*The Workplace Within: Psychodynamics of Organisational Life.*
London: MIT Press.

Huffington, C., & Brunning, H. (Eds.) (1994).
*Internal Consultancy in the Public Sector: Case Studies.* London:
Karnac Books.

Kanter, R. M. (1995).
*World Class: Thriving Locally in the Global Economy.* New
York: Scribners.

Kolb, D. A., Rubin, I. H., & MacIntyre, J. M. (1984).
*Organisational Psychology: An Experiential Approach to
Organizational Behavior.* Englewood Cliffs, NJ: Prentice-Hall.

Legge, K. (1978).
*Power, Innovation & Problem-solving in Management.* New
York: McGraw-Hill.

McCaughan, N., & Palmer, B. (1994).
*Systems Thinking for Harassed Managers.* London: Karnac
Books.

Miller, E. J., & Rice, A. K. (1967).
*Systems of Organisation.* London: Tavistock.

Mohrman, Cummings, & Lawler (1983).
Creating Useful Knowledge. In: R. Kilman & K. Thomas
(Eds.), *Producing Useful Knowledge for Organisations*. New
York: Praeger.

Morgan, G. (1986).
*Images of Organisation*. Beverley Hills, CA/London: Sage.

Morgan, G. (1988).
*Riding the Waves of Change: Developing Managerial
Competencies for a Turbulent World*. San Francisco, CA:
Jossey-Bass.

Nadler, D., & Tushman, M. L. (1977).
A Diagnostic Model for Organisational Behaviour. In: J. R.
Hackman, E. E. Lawler, & L. W. Porter (Eds.), *Perspectives on
Behavior in Organizations*. New York: McGraw-Hill.

Nielsen, E. H. (1984).
*Becoming an O.D. Practitioner*. Englewood Cliffs, NJ:
Prentice-Hall.

Obholzer, A., & Roberts, V. (Eds.) (1994).
*The Unconscious at Work*. London: Routledge.

Schein, E. H. (1969).
*Process Consultation: Its Role in Organizational Development*.
Reading, MA: Addison-Wesley, Series on Organization
Development.

Schmuck, R., & Miles, M. (Eds.) (1976).
*Organization Development in Schools*. San Diego, CA:
University Associates.

Turrill, E. A. (1986).
*Change and Innovation: A Challenge for the NHS*. London:
Institute of Health Services Management.

Watzlawick, P., Weakland, J., & Fisch, R. (1974).
*Change: Principles of Problem Formation and Problem Resolution*.
New York: W. W. Norton.

# APPENDIX 1: FURTHER READING

Bion, W. R.
*Experiences in Groups and Other Papers.* London: Tavistock
Publications, 1961.

Bridges, W.
*Transitions: Making the Most of Change.* London: Nicholas
Brealey, 1995.

Block, P.
*Flawless Consulting: A Guide to Getting Your Expertise Used.*
San Diego, CA: Pfeiffer & Company, 1981.

Blount, A.
Changing Realities in the Firm. *Journal of Strategic & Systemic
Therapies,* 4 (4, Special Organisational Issue), 1985.

Brunning, H., Cole, C., & Huffington, C.
*The Change Directory: Key Issues in Organisational Development
and the Management of Change.* Leicester: The British
Psychological Society, 1990.

Drucker, P.
*Management Tasks, Responsibilities, Practices.* New York:
Harper & Row, 1973.

Emery, F. E., & Trist, E. L.
Socio-Technical Systems. In: C. W. Churchman & M.
Verhulst (Eds.), *Management Science: Models and Techniques,
Vol. 2.* New York: Pergamon, 1960.

Gallensich, J.
*The Profession and Practice of Consultation: A Handbook for
Consultants, Trainees of Consultants and Consumers of
Consultation.* San Francisco, CA: Jossey Bass, 1982.

Handy, C.
*Gods of Management.* London: Hutchinson, 1979.

Handy, C.
*Understanding Organisations*. London: Penguin, 1981.

Handy, C.
*The Age of Unreason*. London: Hutchinson, 1989

Handy, C.
*The Empty Raincoat: Making Sense of the Future*. London: Hutchinson, 1994.

Handy, C.
*Beyond Certainty: The Changing Worlds of Organisations*. London: Hutchinson, 1995.

Handy, C., et al.
*Rethinking the Future*. London: Nicholas Brealey, 1996.

Harrison, M. I.
*Diagnosing Organisations, Methods, Models and Processes, Applied Social Research Methods Series, Vol. 8*. Newbury Park, CA: Sage Publications, 1987.

Hopson, B., Scally, M., & Stafford, K.
*Transitions, the Challenge of Change*. London: Mercury Books, 1992.

Kanter, R. M.
*The Change Masters*. London: Unwin, 1984.

Kubr, M. (Ed.).
*Management Consulting: A Guide to the Profession*. Geneva: International Labour Organisation, 1986.

Lippitt, G., & Lippitt, K.
*The Consulting Process in Action*. La Jolla, CA: University Associates, 1978.

Margerison, C. J.
*Managerial Consulting Skills: A Practical Guide*. Aldershot: Gower, 1988.

Margerison, C. J., & Roden, S.
*Management Development Bibliography*. Buckingham: MCB Publications, 1987.

Page, T.
   *Diary of a Change Agent.* Aldershot: Gower, 1996.

Palazzoli, M. S., et al.
   *The Hidden Games of Organisations.* New York: Pantheon
   Books, 1986.

Peters, T.
   *Thriving on Chaos.* New York: Harper & Row, 1972.

Reed, B. D., & Palmer, B. W. M.
   *An Introduction to Organisational Behaviour.* London: The
   Grubb Institute, 1990.

Senge, P. M.
   *The Fifth Discipline, The Art and Practice of the Learning
   Organisation.* New York: Doubleday, 1990.

Senge, P. M., Roberts, C., Ross, R. B., Smith, B. J., & Kleiner, A.
   *The Fifth Discipline Fieldbook.* London: Nicholas Brearley,
   1995.

Schein, E. H.
   *Process Consultation, Vol. II: Lessons for Managers and
   Consultants.* Reading, MA: Addison-Wesley, Series on
   Organization Development, 1987.

Woodhouse, D., & Pengelly, P.
   *Anxiety and the Dynamics of Collaboration.* Aberdeen:
   Aberdeen University Press, 1991.

Wynne, L. C.
   *Systems Consultation.* New York: Guilford Press, 1986.

# APPENDIX 2: RESOURCES

Journals — Professional associations —
Further training — Miscellaneous

- ## JOURNALS

*Harvard Business Review*
Harvard Business School Publishing Corporation,
60 Harvard Way, Boston, MA 02163, U.S.A.

*Journal of Management Development*
MCB University Press Ltd
Management Development Professionals, 62 Troller Lane,
Bradford, West Yorkshire BD8 9BY
tel (+44) 01274–777–700

*Leadership & Organisational Development Journal*
MCB University Press Ltd
Management Development Professionals, 62 Troller Lane,
Bradford, West Yorkshire BD8 9BY
tel (+44) 01274–777–700

*Management Consultancy Journal*
VNV Business Publications
VNV House, 32–34 Broadwick Street, London SW1A 2HG
tel (+44) 0171–316–9000

*Management, Education & Development*
University of Lancaster
Lancaster LA14YX
tel (+44) 01524–65201

*Management Review*
American Management Association
Box 408, Saranac Lake, NY 122983-0408, U.S.A.

## • PROFESSIONAL ASSOCIATIONS

**American Management Association**
AMA Headquarters
1601 Broadway, New York, NY 10019-7420, U.S.A.

tel 212–903–8073
fax 212–903–8083

**Association for Management Education and Development**
Premier House, 77 Oxford Street, London W1R 1RB

tel (+44) 0171–439–1188

**The British Psychological Society**
Division of Occupational Psychology
St Andrew's House, 48 Princess Road East,
Leicester LE1 7DR

tel (+44) 0116–247–0787

**The Industrial Society**
3 Carlton House Terrace, London SW1 5DG

tel (+44) 0171–839–4300

**Institute of Training and Development**
IPD House
Camp Road, Wimbledon SW19 4UN

tel (+44) 0181–971–9000

**NOWME**
**National Organisation for Women's Management Education**
12a Westbere Road, London NW2

tel (+44) 0171–794–8734

**The Organization Development Institute**
11234 Walnut Ridge Road, Chesterland, OH 44026, U.S.A.

tel 216–461–4333
fax 216–729–9319

## • **FURTHER TRAINING**

**Ashridge Management College**
Berkhamsted, Hertfordshire, HP4 1NS
tel (+44) 01442–843491

**Brunel Institute of Organisation and Social Studies (BIOSS)**
Health Service Centre
BIOSS, Brunel University, Uxbridge, Middlesex UB8 3PH
tel (+44) 01895–270–072

**Cranfield School of Management**
Cranfield, Bedford MK 43 0AL
tel (+44) 01234–751122

**The Grubb Institute**
Cloudesley Street, London N1 OHU
tel (+44) 0171–278–8061

**Innovation Associates Inc.**
Three Speen Street, Suite 140, Framingham, MA 01701, U.S.A.

**Kensington Consultation Centre**
2 Wyril Court, Trenchold Street, London SW8 2TG
tel (+44) 0171–720–7301

**Kings Fund**
11–13 Cavendish Square, London W1M OAN
tel (+44) 0171–307–2400

**The Open Business School**
The Open University
P.O. Box 222, Milton Keynes MK7 6YY
tel (+44) 01908–653449

**Roffey Park Management College**
Forest Road, Horsham, West Sussex RH12 4TD
tel (+44) 01293–851644

**Sloan School of Management**
50 Memorial Drive, Cambridge, MA 02142, U.S.A.

**Sundridge Park Management Centre**
Plaistow Lane, Bromley, Kent BR1 3TP

tel (+44) 0181–313131

**The Tavistock Centre**
120 Belsize Park, London NW3 5BA

tel (+44) 0171–435–7111

**The Tavistock Institute of Human Relations**
30 Tabernacle Street, London EC2A 4DE

tel (+44) 0171–417–0407

- **MISCELLANEOUS**

**Aspire Consultants**
299 Eccleshall Road, Sheffield S11 8NX

tel (+44) 0114–268–0814
fax (+44) 0114–267–1267

**ITS, International Training Services Ltd.**
The Beeches, 37 Parkfield, Coleshill B46 3LD

tel (+44) 01865–466466

# INDEX